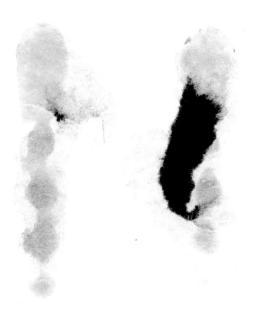

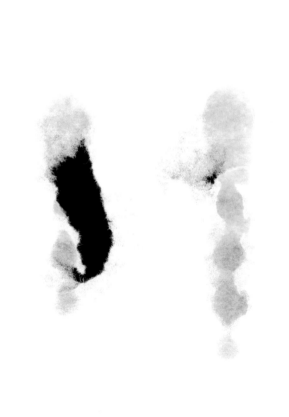

The Ant

Energetic Worker

Luc Gomel

Photos by Rémy Amann and Dominique Stoffel

i◠i Charlesbridge

2

The wood ant's house is made of twigs and pine needles.

Time to wake up

The spring sun shines brightly on a small anthill. The underground chambers and passageways begin to get warm. When the air feels hot enough, a few ants stretch their legs and antennae. Then they wake the rest of the ant colony.

Worker ants make big entrances to their nests to let in heat and air.

Work, work, work

A single large family lives in the anthill. The queen ant is the mother of every ant in the colony. The queen's only job is to lay eggs. Almost all her children are female. They are called workers, and they do everything else the colony needs, including building the anthill, finding food, caring for babies, and protecting the queen.

4

Some ants feed on flower nectar, but they cannot make honey like bees can.

Eggs and larvae fill the ant's nursery.

The queen is the only ant that has a large hump on her back.

Some guards have big heads.

5

🐜 *This larva is becoming an adult. Its eyes turn black, and its body slowly develops.*

🐜 *The ant's eggs are so tiny that they are almost invisible, but cocoons may be small or large, depending on the size of the baby wrapped inside.*

newcomers

The queen lays thousands of eggs, and each egg holds a baby ant that looks like a little white worm when it hatches. The baby is called a larva. It grows very quickly.

When the larva is ready to become an adult, it spins a cocoon around its body and changes shape inside. When the baby comes out, it looks just like an adult ant.

If an enemy threatens the colony, workers immediately carry the cocoons to safety.

The lizard is one of the ant's worst enemies. The badger and the wild boar also destroy anthills.

A guard stretches its antennae, searching for danger.

The ant releases a strong smell to warn of a threat.

Danger!

Ants are always very busy. They work peacefully until they spot a lizard crawling close to the anthill. Guards immediately attack. They swarm over the lizard, biting it and spraying it with poison. Inside the anthill, workers quickly bury the larvae and cocoons in the bottom of the nest to keep them away from the enemy.

The ant stands on its back legs and uses its strong jaws to bite an enemy.

Ready for battle

Whenever two ants meet, they smell each other and touch antennae. They will fight if they are not from the same nest.

The ant's legs often break during a fight.

After a battle ends, the ant cleans itself carefully and checks to make sure its antennae are not damaged.

Many ants working together can kill a grasshopper, even though it is much bigger than they are.

Ants attack their enemies in many ways. Most ants bite with their strong pincerlike jaws, called mandibles. Some species spray poisonous acid on their victims, and others sting their prey with a stinger like a bee's.

This ant bites a caterpillar, then squirts acid into the wound.

11

 An ant strokes the back of an aphid to release a drop of sweet syrup from its body.

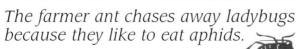 *The farmer ant chases away ladybugs because they like to eat aphids.*

These two ants are sharing food.

Farming

Just as humans raise cows for milk, some ants raise aphids for plant syrup. The aphid often sucks too much juice from a plant. The excess syrup falls in small drops from the aphid's body. The farmer ant sucks up the syrup and stores it in a cavity in front of its stomach. Then the ant returns to the colony to share the liquid with its family.

This ant has eaten a lot of food and has a swollen belly.

Princes and princesses

In the spring, flying ants are born in the ant colony. Half of them are princesses, who may become queens someday. The other half are princes. They are the only males in the colony, and their only job is to mate with the princesses. These ants wait inside the anthill until their wedding day.

A princess and a worker communicate with their antennae and body odors.

Only ants born with wings can mate. Females are much bigger than males.

The wedding flight

On a warm day, the flying ants finally leave the anthill and take to the air. There are so many, they look like a thick cloud in the sky. The ants mate during the flight. Afterwards, the males die, and the females' wings fall off. The princesses are now ready to be queens, and they will never fly again.

Swallows often hunt the flying ants.

A new family

A young queen digs a hole in the ground and disappears to lay the first eggs of a new ant colony. The queen must spend several months alone until her first babies are born. She cannot get any food for herself, so she lives off the nutrients in her wing muscles. Her first children will find food for her and build an anthill for their new colony.

As soon as a new queen loses her wings, she disappears underground.

The worker ants build an anthill as soon as they become adults.

Pest or protector?

The ant can be a nuisance when it gets into a person's house, but it is an important protector of the environment. The ant eats decaying plants and animals and also living insects that destroy trees. The ant's tunnels help loosen the earth, making it easier for plants to grow.

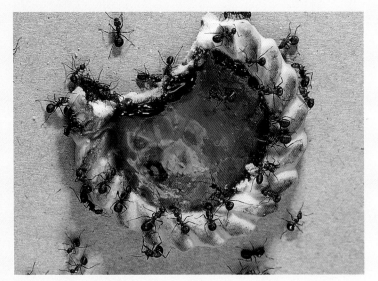

 These ants are feasting on a leftover cookie.

Living with ants

Ants are always looking for food. They often raid people's kitchens and raise aphids on the plants in people's gardens. It can be hard to get rid of an unwanted ant colony. Most ants hide deep in the ground if they sense danger and come out only when they feel safe again.

20

Watch and learn

Ants are incredible to watch under a magnifying glass or in an insect aquarium. You can also observe them near their nests or build an ant farm at home. Many museums display giant ant colonies that you can watch through big windows. Ants can teach us about cooperation, hard work, and organization.

People can learn a lot from watching the ant.

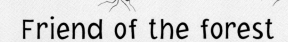

Friend of the forest

Wood ants kill and eat caterpillars. The ants help save many trees that otherwise would have been destroyed by caterpillars munching on the leaves. Humans must take care never to kill wood ants or harm their nests on the forest floor.

This red wood ant is attacking a caterpillar.

21

harvester ant

A very big family

The ant is an insect. It has six legs, and its body is divided into three sections. Scientists think that there are more than 12,000 different species of ants, but there may be many more still undiscovered in tropical forests around the world. All ants live in colonies, but each species has its own unique way of life.

The **harvester ant** eats only grain, seeds, and sometimes a few insects. It lives in warm areas where heat from the sun helps turn the starch in seeds into sugar that the ant can eat. Many people think harvesters are pests because they often eat grass seed, destroying yards and lawns.

The **slaver ant** often steals cocoons from other ant colonies. When the babies hatch, the slaver forces them to work in its own colony. The slaver ant is a fierce warrior and fights constantly. It is small but very strong.

slaver ant

22

The **weaver ant** builds its home out of leaves in the trees of southern Asia and the Pacific Islands. Several weaver ants work together to push two leaves next to one another. Then the ants sew the leaves together with silk thread made by larvae. The adults hold the babies gently in their mandibles.

weaver ant

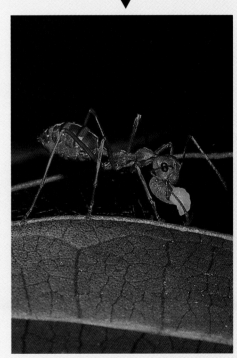

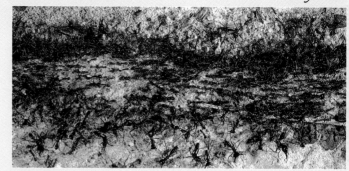

army ant

The **army ant** does not build a permanent home. It lives in the forests of South America in large colonies. Thousands of army ants travel together in a gigantic swarm, eating everything in their path. People often leave their villages until the ants have passed through. The army ant's curved, sharp mandibles make its bite very painful.

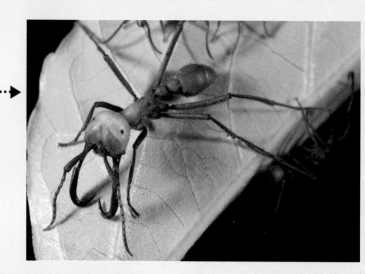

Some South American peoples use the army ant's mandibles to hold two sides of a cut together until it heals.

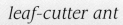 *leaf-cutter ant*

The **leaf-cutter ant** actually grows its own food. It cuts leaves and flowers from plants and carries them underground. Then it chews the plants into a paste from which delicious fungus will grow. The leaf-cutter lives in Central and South America and in the southern United States.

This ant is carrying a flower underground piece by piece.

25

A Quick Quiz about Ants:

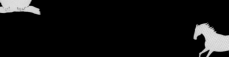

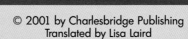

© 2000 by Editions Milan under the title La fourmi, travailleuse infatigable
300 rue Léon-Joulin, 31101 Toulouse Cedex 100, France
French series editor, Valérie Tracqui

Published by Charlesbridge Publishing
85 Main Street, Watertown, MA 02472
(617) 926-0329 • www.charlesbridge.com

Library of Congress Cataloging-in-Publication Data
Gomel, Luc.
[Fourmi. English]
The ant : energetic worker / Luc Gomel.
p. cm. — (Face to face)
ISBN 1-57091-451-6 (hardcover)
1. Ants—Juvenile literature. [1. Ants.] I. Title. II. Face to face (Watertown, Mass.)
QL568.F7 G6313 2001
595.79′6-dc21   00-063890

Printed in Singapore
10 9 8 7 6 5 4 3 2 1

4115

PLEASE SHARE YOUR THOUGHTS
ON THIS BOOK

comments:	comments:
comments:	comments:
comments:	comments:
comments:	comments:
comments:	comments:
comments:	comments: